Vegetarian One Pot Cookbo

Delicious And Easy V~~~~~
Pot Meal Recipes

Table of Contents

Introduction

This vegetarian one pot cookbook wide selection of delicious soup, stew and chili recipes you can easily make with one pot. This vegetarian one pot cookbook is great if you are too busy or too lazy to make a complicated meal. You simply have to add the ingredients into a pot and cook!

All of these recipes are vegetarian and 100% meat free, they also taste great. We hope you enjoy these vegetarian one pot meal recipes and good luck!

Chapter 1: Vegetarian Chili And Stew Recipes

Spicy Vegetarian Corn And Bean Chili

Ingredients

1 tablespoon olive oil

1/2 medium onion, chopped

2 bay leaves

1 teaspoon ground cumin

2 tablespoons dried oregano

1 tablespoon salt

2 stalks celery, chopped

2 green bell peppers, chopped

2 jalapeno peppers, chopped

3 cloves garlic, chopped

2 (4 ounce) cans chopped green chile peppers, drained

2 (12 ounce) packages vegetarian burger crumbles

3 (28 ounce) cans whole peeled tomatoes, crushed

1/4 cup chili powder

1 tablespoon ground black pepper

1 (15 ounce) can kidney beans, drained

1 (15 ounce) can garbanzo beans, drained

1 (15 ounce) can black beans

1 (15 ounce) can whole kernel corn

Directions

Heat the olive oil in a large pot over medium heat. Stir in the onion, and season with bay leaves, cumin, oregano, and salt.

Cook and stir until onion is tender, then mix in the celery, green bell peppers, jalapeño peppers, garlic, and green chile peppers.

When vegetables are heated through, mix in the vegetarian burger crumbles. Reduce heat to low, cover pot, and simmer 5 minutes.

Mix the tomatoes into the pot. Season chili with chili powder and pepper. Stir in the kidney beans, garbanzo beans, and black beans. Bring to a boil, reduce heat to low, and simmer 45 minutes.

Stir in the corn, and continue cooking 5 minutes before serving.

Chickpea Stew

Ingredients
1 tablespoon olive oil

1 small onion, chopped

2 cloves garlic, minced

2 teaspoons ground cumin

2 teaspoons ground coriander

1/2 teaspoon cayenne pepper, or to taste

1 teaspoon garam masala

1/2 teaspoon curry powder

1 pinch salt

3 potatoes, cut into 1/2-inch cubes

1 (14.5 ounce) can diced tomatoes, undrained

1 cup tomato sauce

1 cup golden raisins

water, or enough to cover

1 (14.5 ounce) can chickpeas, drained and rinsed

1 bunch kale, ribs removed, chopped

1/2 cup chopped fresh cilantro

Directions

Heat the olive oil in a large pot over medium heat; cook the onion and garlic in the hot oil until the onions are translucent, 5 to 7 minutes. Stir the cumin, coriander, cayenne pepper, garam masala, curry powder, and salt into the onion and garlic; cook together until fragrant, about 1 minute.

Add the potatoes, diced tomatoes, tomato sauce, and raisins to the pot. Pour enough water over the mixture to cover; bring to a simmer and cook until the potatoes are soft, 10 to 15 minutes.

Add the chickpeas and kale to the pot; simmer until the kale wilts, about 3 minutes. Sprinkle the cilantro over the stew and immediately remove the pot from the heat.

Tortilla Stew

Ingredients

1 (19 ounce) can green enchilada sauce

1 1/2 cups water

1 cube vegetable bouillon

1/2 teaspoon garlic powder

1/4 teaspoon chili powder

1/4 teaspoon ground cumin

1 (15 ounce) can pinto beans, drained and rinsed

1/2 (16 ounce) can diced tomatoes

1 cup frozen corn

1/2 cup vegetarian chicken substitute, diced (optional)

4 (6 inch) corn tortillas, torn into strips

1 tablespoon chopped fresh cilantro

salt and pepper to taste

Directions

In a pot, mix the enchilada sauce and water. Dissolve the bouillon cube in the liquid, and season with garlic powder, chile powder, and cumin. Bring to a boil, and reduce heat to low.

Mix in the beans, tomatoes, and corn. Simmer until heated through. Mix in vegetarian chicken and tortillas, and cook until heated through.

Stir in cilantro, and season with salt and pepper to serve.

Quinoa Chipotle Chili

Ingredients

1 cup uncooked quinoa, rinsed

2 cups water

1 tablespoon vegetable oil

1 onion, chopped

4 cloves garlic, chopped

1 tablespoon chili powder

1 tablespoon ground cumin

1 (28 ounce) can crushed tomatoes

2 (19 ounce) cans black beans, rinsed and drained

1 green bell pepper, chopped

1 red bell pepper, chopped

1 zucchini, chopped

1 jalapeno pepper, seeded and minced

1 tablespoon minced chipotle peppers in adobo sauce

1 teaspoon dried oregano

salt and ground black pepper to taste

1 cup frozen corn

1/4 cup chopped fresh cilantro

Directions

Bring the quinoa and water to a boil in a saucepan over high heat. Reduce heat to medium-low, cover, and simmer until the quinoa is tender, and the water has been absorbed, about 15 to 20 minutes; set aside.

Meanwhile, heat the vegetable oil in a large pot over medium heat. Stir in the onion, and cook until the onion softens and turns translucent, about 5 minutes.

Add the garlic, chili powder, and cumin; cook and stir 1 minute to release the flavors. Stir in the tomatoes, black beans, green bell pepper, red bell pepper, zucchini, jalapeno pepper, chipotle pepper, and oregano. Season to taste with salt and pepper.

Bring to a simmer over high heat, then reduce heat to medium-low, cover, and simmer 20 minutes.

After 20 minutes, stir in the reserved quinoa and corn. Cook to reheat the corn for 5 minutes. Remove from the heat, and stir in the cilantro to serve.

Sweet Potato Chili

Ingredients

2 pounds orange-fleshed sweet potatoes, peeled and cut into cubes

1/2 teaspoon ground dried chipotle pepper

1/2 teaspoon salt

2 tablespoons olive oil, divided

1 onion, diced

4 cloves garlic, minced

1 red bell pepper, diced

1 jalapeno pepper, sliced

2 tablespoons ancho chile powder, or to taste

1 tablespoon ground cumin

1/4 teaspoon dried oregano

1 (28 ounce) can diced tomatoes

1 cup water, or more as needed

1 tablespoon cornmeal

1 teaspoon salt, or to taste

1 teaspoon white sugar

1 teaspoon unsweetened cocoa powder

2 (15 ounce) cans black beans, rinsed and drained

1 pinch cayenne pepper, or to taste

1/2 cup sour cream, for garnish (optional)

1/4 cup chopped fresh cilantro, for garnish (optional)

Directions

Preheat oven to 400F. Line a baking sheet with parchment paper or a silicone baking mat.

Combine sweet potatoes, chipotle pepper, 1/2 teaspoon salt, and 1 tablespoon olive oil in a large bowl and toss to coat. Spread sweet potatoes on the prepared baking sheet in a single layer.

Roast sweet potatoes in the preheated oven until the outside is crunchy and inside is tender, 20 to 25 minutes. Allow to cool to room temperature.

Cook and stir remaining 1 tablespoon olive oil, onion, garlic, red bell pepper, jalapeno pepper, ancho chile powder, cumin, and dried oregano together in a large pot or Dutch oven over medium heat. Cook and stir until onion is softened, about 5 minutes.

Pour tomatoes and water into the onion mixture and bring to a simmer. Add cornmeal, 1 teaspoon salt, sugar, and cocoa powder. Bring to a simmer, stirring constantly, reduce heat to low and simmer for 30 minutes.

Stir black beans and cooled sweet potatoes into the onion-tomato mixture. Add more water if mixture is too thick. Simmer until heated through, about 15 minutes. Season with salt and cayenne pepper to taste.

Serve topped with sour cream and cilantro.

Savoury Mexican Stew

Ingredients

5 medium potatoes, peeled and cubed

2 carrots, chopped

1 stalk celery, chopped

4 1/2 cups water

4 cubes vegetable bouillon

1 tablespoon olive oil

1 large onion, diced

4 cloves garlic, minced

1 tablespoon chili powder

1 tablespoon cumin

1 1/2 tablespoons seasoned salt

1 (29 ounce) can hominy, drained

1 (28 ounce) can diced tomatoes with green chile peppers

salt and pepper to taste

Directions

Place the potatoes, carrots, and celery in a pot with enough lightly salted water to cover, and bring to a boil. Cook about 10 minutes, until slightly tender. Drain, and set aside.

Place the 4 1/2 cups water and vegetable bouillon cubes in a pot. Bring to a boil, and cook until bouillon cubes have dissolved. Remove from heat, and set aside.

Heat the olive oil in a large pot. Saute the onion and garlic until tender. Season with chili powder, cumin, and seasoned salt. Mix in the potatoes, carrots, and celery.

Cook and stir about 2 minutes, until heated through. Mix in the water and dissolved bouillon cube mixture, hominy, and diced tomatoes with green chiles.

Bring to a boil, reduce heat, and simmer 45 minutes. Season with salt and pepper to taste.

Spinach and Barley Stew

Ingredients

1 cup uncooked pearl barley

3 cups water

1 teaspoon olive oil

1 cup chopped yellow onion

2 cloves garlic, minced

1/2 teaspoon dried rosemary

3/4 cup small fresh mushrooms

1 cup chopped yellow bell pepper

2 tablespoons white wine

1 (15.5 ounce) can white beans, drained and rinsed

1 (14.5 ounce) can Italian-style diced tomatoes, drained

2 cups fresh spinach

1 pinch red pepper flakes

Directions

Bring the barley and water to a boil in a pot. Cover, reduce heat to low, and simmer 30 minutes, or until tender.

Heat the olive oil in a large pot over medium heat, and cook the onion and garlic until tender. Season with rosemary.

Mix the mushrooms, yellow bell pepper, and wine into the pot, and cook 5 minutes. Stir in the cooked barley, beans, tomatoes, and spinach.

Season with red pepper flakes. Continue cooking 10 minutes, or until spinach is wilted.

Chipotle Sweet Potato Chile

Ingredients

1 tablespoon plus 2 teaspoons extra-virgin olive oil

1 medium-large sweet potato, peeled and diced

1 large onion, diced

4 cloves garlic, minced

2 tablespoons chili powder

4 teaspoons ground cumin

½ teaspoon ground chipotle chile (see Note)

¼ teaspoon salt

2½ cups water

2 15-ounce cans black beans, rinsed

1 14-ounce can diced tomatoes

4 teaspoons lime juice

½ cup chopped fresh cilantro

Directions

Heat oil in a Dutch oven over medium-high heat. Add sweet potato and onion and cook, stirring often, until the onion is beginning to soften, about 4 minutes.

Add garlic, chili powder, cumin, chipotle and salt and cook, stirring constantly, for 30 seconds. Add water and bring to a simmer. Cover, reduce heat to maintain a gentle simmer and cook until the sweet potato is tender, 10 to 12 minutes.

Add beans, tomatoes and lime juice; increase heat to high and return to a simmer, stirring often.

Reduce heat and simmer until slightly reduced, about 5 minutes. Remove from heat and stir in cilantro.

Squash And Bean Stew

Ingredients

3 tablespoons olive oil

1 large white onion, diced

1 tablespoon ground cinnamon

2 tablespoons chili powder

4 cloves crushed garlic

1 tablespoon cumin seeds, toasted

2 tablespoons fresh lemon juice

4 large tomatoes - peeled, seeded, and coarsely chopped

1 medium acorn squash, peeled and diced

1 cup pinto beans, cooked or canned

1 cup water

salt and pepper to taste

Directions

In a large heavy-bottomed pot, heat olive oil and saute the onion for a few minutes. Add the cinnamon and chili powder and continue to saute for another 2 minutes.

Mix in the garlic and cumin seeds, saute for 2 minutes more before adding lemon juice and the tomatoes. Mix thoroughly so the stew doesn't get too chunky.

Stir the squash, pinto beans and water into the stew. Season with salt and pepper to taste. Let the stew simmer for 1 hour, or until squash is tender.

Stirring occasionally throughout the cooking hour, and add more water if necessary. The finished stew should have a nice, thick stewy texture.

Heat a large skillet over a medium-high heat. Place one piece of pita bread at a time into the skillet.

When one side of the pita bread gets hot, flip the bread over and heat the other side; approximately 1 minute of cooking per side. Serve the stew with the heated pita bread.

Moroccan Stew

Ingredients

1 tablespoon olive oil

1 small onion, chopped

2 cloves garlic, minced

2 teaspoons ground cumin

2 teaspoons ground coriander

1/2 teaspoon cayenne pepper, or to taste

1 teaspoon garam masala

1/2 teaspoon curry powder

1 pinch salt

3 potatoes, cut into 1/2-inch cubes

1 (14.5 ounce) can diced tomatoes, undrained

1 cup tomato sauce

1 cup golden raisins

water, or enough to cover

1 (14.5 ounce) can chickpeas, drained and rinsed

1 bunch kale, ribs removed, chopped

1/2 cup chopped fresh cilantro

Directions

Heat the olive oil in a large pot over medium heat; cook the onion and garlic in the hot oil until the onions are translucent, 5 to 7 minutes. Stir the cumin, coriander, cayenne pepper, garam masala, curry powder, and salt into the onion and garlic; cook together until fragrant, about 1 minute.

Add the potatoes, diced tomatoes, tomato sauce, and raisins to the pot. Pour enough water over the mixture to cover; bring to a simmer and cook until the potatoes are soft, 10 to 15 minutes.

Add the chickpeas and kale to the pot; simmer until the kale wilts, about 3 minutes.

Sprinkle the cilantro over the stew and immediately remove the pot from the heat.

Tofu Chili

Ingredients

1/2 (12 ounce) package extra firm tofu

1 teaspoon chili powder

1 clove garlic, minced

2 tablespoons vegetable oil

1/2 cup onion, chopped

2 stalks celery, chopped

1/2 cup whole kernel corn, undrained

1 (15.25 ounce) can kidney beans, undrained

1 (14.5 ounce) can stewed tomatoes, undrained

1 quart water

Directions

In a medium bowl, crumble the tofu and toss with the chili powder and garlic.

Heat the oil in a large saucepan over medium heat, and saute the onion and celery until tender. Stir in the tofu mixture. Continue cooking about 5 minutes over low heat.

Mix in the corn, kidney beans, and stewed tomatoes. Add water and bring to a boil. Reduce heat to low and simmer about 50 minutes.

Hearty Bean And Corn Stew

Ingredients

1 cup dried pinto beans

1 cup dry black beans

1 cup dry garbanzo beans

1 tablespoon olive oil

1 onion, diced

4 cloves garlic, crushed

1 teaspoon ground cumin

1 (14.5 ounce) can crushed tomatoes

2 cups fresh corn kernels

1/2 teaspoon ground cinnamon

salt and pepper to taste

cayenne pepper to taste

Directions

Rinse and sort pinto beans, black beans and garbanzo beans. Place in a large bowl and cover with water. Soak overnight.

Drain beans and place in a large pot; cover with water. Bring to a boil and cook for 1 hour, or until beans are tender. It may be necessary to add more water during cooking to prevent drying out or scorching.

Heat oil in a small saucepan over medium-high heat. Saute onion and garlic until onion is transparent. Stir in cumin. To the beans add the onions, garlic and crushed tomatoes.

Simmer for 20 minutes. Stir in corn and cinnamon; cook 15 minutes more. Season with salt, pepper and cayenne to taste before serving.

Easy Tofu Curry

Ingredients

2 tablespoons curry powder, preferably Madras

½ teaspoon salt

¼ teaspoon freshly ground pepper

1 14-ounce package extra-firm or firm water-packed tofu

4 teaspoons canola oil, divided

1 large delicata squash (about 1 pound), halved, seeded and cut into 1-inch cubes

1 medium onion, halved and sliced

2 teaspoons grated fresh ginger

1 14-ounce can "lite" coconut milk

1 teaspoon light brown sugar

8 cups coarsely chopped kale or chard, tough stems removed

1 tablespoon lime juice, plus more to taste

Directions

Combine curry powder, salt and pepper in a small bowl. Blot tofu dry with a paper towel and cut into 1-inch cubes; toss the tofu in a medium bowl with 1 teaspoon of the spice mixture.

Heat 2 teaspoons oil in a large nonstick skillet over medium-high heat. Add the tofu and cook, stirring every 2 minutes, until browned, 6 to 8 minutes total. Transfer to a plate.

Heat the remaining 2 teaspoons oil over medium-high heat. Add squash, onion, ginger and the remaining spice mixture; cook, stirring, until the vegetables are lightly browned, 4 to 5 minutes. Add coconut milk and brown sugar; bring to a boil.

Add half the kale (or chard) and cook, stirring, until slightly wilted, about 1 minute. Stir in the rest of the greens and cook, stirring, for 1 minute.

Return the tofu to the pan, cover and cook, stirring once or twice, until the squash and greens are tender, 3 to 5 minutes more. Remove from the heat and stir in lime juice.

Potato Stew

Ingredients

3 quarts water

8 large potatoes, peeled and sliced

4 large carrots, diced

2 stalks celery, chopped

2 small onions, chopped

1/3 cup butter

2 tablespoons all-purpose flour

1 1/2 teaspoons salt

1 teaspoon ground black pepper

1/4 teaspoon paprika

2 cups heavy cream

Directions

In a large saucepan over medium heat, heat the water and stir in the potatoes, carrots and celery.

Cook 15 minutes, or until tender but firm. Remove from heat. Drain and set aside, reserving liquid.

Place the onions and butter in the large saucepan. Over medium heat, slowly cook and stir 10 minutes, or until the onions are tender. Mix in the flour, salt, pepper, paprika and heavy cream.

Mix in the potato mixture. Continue cooking and stirring, adding the reserved liquid a tablespoon at a time, until the mixture has reached a desired consistency.

One Pot Quinoa and Vegetables

Ingredients

1 cup quinoa, rinsed

2 cup water

4 medium carrots, chopped

1 zucchini, chopped

8 spears fresh asparagus, chopped

1 tbsp rice wine vinegar

2 tbsp olive oil

1 tsp fresh thyme, leaves removed from stem

black pepper to taste

Directions

Place water in a small covered saucepan. Bring to a boil. Add quinoa and stir. Reduce heat to a simmer and replace lid. Simmer for 11-12 minutes, or until water is absorbed.

Steam the vegetables for 3-4 minutes, either in the microwave or in a small covered pot with 1/2 inch water.

Meanwhile, prepare the vinaigrette. Place the vinegar and thyme in a small bowl, then whisk in the oil. Once the quinoa is cooked, fluff it with a fork.

Place 3/4 cup of quinoa on each plate. Arrange a quarter of the vegetables over the quinoa and top with about 2 teaspoons of the vinaigrette.

Chapter 2: Vegetarian One Pot Soup Recipes

Salsa Soup

Ingredients

2 (15 ounce) cans black beans, drained and rinsed

1 1/2 cups vegetable broth

1 cup chunky salsa

1 teaspoon ground cumin

4 tablespoons sour cream

2 tablespoons thinly sliced green onion

Directions

In an electric food processor or blender, combine beans, broth, salsa, and cumin. Blend until fairly smooth.

Heat the bean mixture in a saucepan over medium heat until thoroughly heated.

Ladle soup into 4 individual bowls, and top each bowl with 1 tablespoon of the sour cream and 1/2 tablespoon green onion.

Kale Soup

Ingredients

2 tablespoons olive oil

1 yellow onion, chopped

2 tablespoons chopped garlic

1 bunch kale, stems removed and leaves chopped

8 cups water

6 cubes vegetable bouillon

1 (15 ounce) can diced tomatoes

6 white potatoes, peeled and cubed

2 (15 ounce) cans cannellini beans (drained if desired)

1 tablespoon Italian seasoning

2 tablespoons dried parsley

salt and pepper to taste

Directions

Heat the olive oil in a large soup pot; cook the onion and garlic until soft. Stir in the kale and cook until wilted, about 2 minutes.

Stir in the water, vegetable bouillon, tomatoes, potatoes, beans, Italian seasoning, and parsley.

Simmer soup on medium heat for 25 minutes, or until potatoes are cooked through. Season with salt and pepper to taste.

Mushroom and Bean Soup

Ingredients

2 tbsp canola oil

1 medium onion, thinly sliced

1 clove garlic

2 vegetarian bacon strips

3 stalks celery, chopped

1 cup mushrooms

1 bay leaf

8 cup water

Salt & Pepper to taste

1 can navy beans (14oz.), drained and rinsed

4 cups fresh or frozen spinach

Directions

Brown onions, vegetarian bacon, celery and garlic in canola oil in large soup pot.

Continue to brown until onions are caramelized. Add mushrooms and sauté until mushrooms release their liquids.

Add water, salt, pepper and bay leaf. Simmer for 10 minutes. Add beans to heat through. Add in spinach just before serving.

Spinach and White Bean Soup

Ingredients

2 teaspoons olive oil

4 leeks, bulb only, chopped

2 cloves garlic, chopped

2 (16 ounce) cans fat-free chicken broth

2 (16 ounce) cans cannellini beans, rinsed and drained

2 bay leaves

2 teaspoons ground cumin

1/2 cup whole wheat couscous

2 cups packed fresh spinach

salt and pepper to taste

Directions

Heat olive oil in a large saucepan or soup pot over medium heat. Add the leeks and garlic; saute until tender, about 5 minutes.

Stir in the chicken broth, cannellini beans, bay leaves and cumin. Bring to a boil, then reduce the heat to low, and stir in the couscous.

Cover, and simmer for 5 minutes. Stir in spinach and season with salt and pepper.

Squash And Red Lentil Soup

Ingredients

1 tablespoon peanut oil

1 small onion, chopped

1 tablespoon minced fresh ginger root

1 clove garlic, chopped

1 pinch fenugreek seeds

1 cup dry red lentils

1 cup butternut squash - peeled, seeded, and cubed

1/3 cup finely chopped fresh cilantro

2 cups water

1/2 (14 ounce) can coconut milk

2 tablespoons tomato paste

1 teaspoon curry powder

1 pinch cayenne pepper

1 pinch ground nutmeg

salt and pepper to taste

Directions

Heat the oil in a large pot over medium heat, and cook the onion, ginger, garlic, and fenugreek until onion is tender.

Mix the lentils, squash, and cilantro into the pot. Stir in the water, coconut milk, and tomato paste.

Season with curry powder, cayenne pepper, nutmeg, salt, and pepper.

Bring to a boil, reduce heat to low, and simmer 30 minutes, or until lentils and squash are tender.

Hot and Sour Tofu Soup

Ingredients

1/4 cup vegetable broth

4 cloves garlic, minced

2 whole scallions, chopped

2 cups vegetable broth

1 cup water

1 1/2 cups shiitake mushroom pieces

1/2 block soft tofu, small sized pieces

2 ounces dry rice noodles

1/2 cup baby bok choy leaves

1 tbsp coriander

1 tsp cumin

1 tsp black pepper

2 tbsp light soy sauce

2 tbsp red wine vinegar

Directions

Saute your garlic and scallions in 1/4 cup vegetable broth for about 10 minutes on medium heat. Then add the rest of the broth, mushroom pieces, tofu pieces, bok choy and spices - coriander, cumin, black pepper and simmer for approximately 10 minutes.

Add rice noodles and simmer for approximately 20 minutes until noodles are soft.

Finally add soy sauce and vinegar and serve immediately.

Savory Cabbage and Tomato Soup

Ingredients

1/4 cup butter or margarine

1 onion, chopped

3 potatoes, diced

3 stalks celery, chopped

3 cloves garlic, minced

4 cups water

2 cubes chicken bouillon

1/2 head cabbage, finely chopped

1 (28 ounce) can whole tomatoes with basil, undrained and chopped

1/2 cup ketchup

1 teaspoon hot sauce

1 teaspoon Italian seasoning

Directions

Melt the butter in a large pot over medium-high heat. Cook and stir the onion, potatoes, celery, and garlic in the melted butter until the onion and celery are translucent, 5 to 7 minutes.

Pour the water over the vegetable mixture; stir the chicken bouillon into the liquid until dissolved. Bring the mixture to a boil; cook at a boil until the potatoes are fork-tender, about 5 minutes.

Stir the cabbage into the boiling liquid. Reduce heat to medium. Add the tomatoes with juices, ketchup, hot sauce, and Italian seasoning; stir to combine.

Allow the mixture to simmer until the flavors have a chance to mix, about 15 minutes.

Classic French Onion Soup

Ingredients

1/4 cup butter

8 onions, sliced

1 quart vegetable broth

1 1/2 cups white wine

salt and pepper to taste

6 slices baguette

2 cups shredded mozzarella cheese

Directions

Melt butter in a large pot over medium heat. Saute onions until deep brown, about 20 minutes.

Stir in broth and wine, using a wooden spoon to scrape the bottom of the pot. Season with salt and pepper. Cook until heated through.

Preheat oven on broiler setting. Ladle soup into heatproof serving bowls. Top each bowl with a slice of bread, and sprinkle with cheese. Place under a hot broiler until cheese is melted and slightly browned.

Carrot Soup

Ingredients

2 tablespoons extra virgin olive oil

1 small onion, minced

1 small carrot, peeled and thinly sliced

1 celery rib, thinly sliced

1/2 teaspoon dried tarragon

2 cups vegetable broth

1/2 cup dry white wine

Directions

Heat the oil in a medium saucepan over medium-high heat. Saute onions until tender, approximately 5 minutes.

Slowly stir in carrots, celery, and tarragon, and continue cooking another 5 minutes, or until carrots are tender.

Stir in vegetable broth and wine, and bring to a boil. Reduce to a simmer, and continue cooking 15 minutes longer. Serve hot.

Spicy Tortilla Soup

Ingredients

1 tbsp extra light olive oil

1 can white beans

1.5 cups frozen corn

1 cup frozen green beans

1 cup chopped onion

1 tbsp garlic powder

4 cups vegetarian chicken broth (or vegetable broth)

2 tbsp ground cumin

1 tsp garlic salt

1 can diced tomatoes and green chilies

2.5 oz of tortilla chips

Directions

Saute onion in olive oil.

Add all ingredients and bring to a simmer for 15-20 minutes. Serve with tortilla chips sprinkled on top.

Lentil Vegetable Soup

Ingredients

2 1/2 tablespoons vegetable oil

1 fresh green onions, chopped

1 carrot, chopped

1 parsnip, sliced

1 stalk celery, chopped

1 potato, cubed

1 leek, chopped

1 cup dry lentils, rinsed

1 (14.5 ounce) can diced tomatoes

3 cups vegetable broth

2 bay leaves

1 dash soy sauce

1 dash Worcestershire sauce

1/2 cup red wine

Directions

In a large saucepan over medium heat, combine the oil, onions, carrot, parsnip, celery, potato and leek.

Stir well for 5 minutes, or until onion is translucent. Add the lentils, tomatoes with liquid, stock, bay leaves, soy sauce, Worcestershire sauce and wine.

Bring to a boil and reduce heat to low.

Cover and simmer for 30 minutes or until lentils are tender. Remove the bay leaves and add the fresh coriander or fresh parsley to taste.

Wild Rice Curry Soup

Ingredients

1 cup uncooked wild rice

1/4 cup butter

1 onion, chopped

2 1/2 cups sliced fresh mushrooms

1/2 cup chopped celery

1/2 cup all-purpose flour

6 cups vegetable broth

2 cups half-and-half

2/3 cup dry sherry

1/2 teaspoon salt

1/2 teaspoon white pepper

1/2 teaspoon curry powder

1/2 teaspoon dry mustard

1/2 teaspoon paprika

1/2 teaspoon dried chervil

1 tablespoon chopped fresh parsley, for garnish

Directions

In a saucepan bring water to a boil. Add rice and stir. Reduce heat, cover and simmer until tender, about 40 minutes.

Heat butter in a large saucepan over medium heat. Saute onion until golden brown; add mushrooms and celery. Cook 2 minutes, stirring constantly.

Reduce heat to low; stir in flour and cook, stirring constantly, until mixture is bubbly. Gradually add broth; increase heat to medium-high and bring to a boil. Boil, stirring, for 1 minute.

Reduce heat to low and add cooked rice, half and half, sherry, salt, white pepper, curry powder, dry mustard, paprika and chervil. Simmer until heated through.

Serve hot and garnish with parsley.

Printed in Poland
by Amazon Fulfillment
Poland Sp. z o.o., Wrocław